Prayers
of Hope *for*
the
Brokenhearted

JILL KELLY

HARVEST HOUSE PUBLISHERS

EUGENE, OREGON

Published in association with the literary agency of Wolgemuth & Associates

All photos © www.BrodyWheeler.com

Cover by Left Coast Design, Portland, Oregon

PRAYERS OF HOPE FOR THE BROKENHEARTED
Copyright © 2010 by Jill Kelly
Published by Harvest House Publishers
Eugene, Oregon 97402
www.harvesthousepublishers.com

ISBN 978-0-7369-2933-2

Printed in China

10 11 12 13 14 15 16 17 / RDS-NI / 10 9 8 7 6 5 4 3 2 1

Jesus, thank You for holding my heart.
You are everything to me.

Thank You...

"I thank my God every time I remember you. In all my prayers for all of you, I always pray with joy because of your partnership in the gospel from the first day until now...It is right for me to feel this way about all of you, since I have you in my heart" (Philippians 1:3-7).

A book like this doesn't just happen. It takes a team to accomplish great things. And that's exactly what this book journey has been like for me...teamwork.

Harvest House is a team I pray I will have the pleasure and honor of working with for years to come. Bob Hawkins Jr., LaRae Weikert, Kim Moore, and so many others have blessed me in countless ways, and I'm grateful. Kim, can we do this again? Because you're an old friend now.

Robert Wolgemuth—you're great. I'm so thankful that God brought the Kellys and Wolgemuths together. Certainly a combination for His kingdom...and great fun too.

Rick Kern—as always, you rock! Thank you for always being there no matter what.

Pastor Matt—thank you for reading through these prayers with a biblical eye. We love you and your family.

To my family...Jim, Erin, Cam...Mom, Dad, Jack, Kim—I love you more than words can say.

Hunter James Kelly—I thank God for breaking my heart through your incredible life. He holds me together as I wait to see you again.

Contents

My Heart to Yours

*W*hile I sat doing my quiet time one very cold January morning, an overwhelming sense of urgency came over me that ultimately led to this book of prayers.

Life is hard.

Riddled with disappointment and heartbreak, life's pilgrimage often brings us face-to-face with trials and sorrowful times. Tragedy can immobilize and weaken us, catching us completely off guard as it threatens to suck the joy of life right out of us.

And if we are honest, giving up appears more attractive every day.

Yet when we are at our weakest, there is a God who is strong and mighty to save.

I have had the very difficult yet incredible privilege of getting to know many families with critically ill children. My heart hurts for them as they struggle to endure. And while the gift of taking care of a special-needs child is immeasurable, the brokenness it brings is very real. I know. I've been there.

All too often, while taking care of my precious son, Hunter, I found myself speechless before God. I didn't know what to pray or how to pray. I wanted to express the frustration and fears in my heart in a way that would bring healing and hope. What I have come to know is this—God is listening, and even unspoken cries are heard.

It is my hope that these prayers will help you to express what you cannot seem to put into words. Ultimately, I pray that God will inspire and encourage you to pour out your heart before Him in a way that will bring deep healing and freedom.

Prayers of Hope for the Brokenhearted is an opportunity to spend time with the God who sees and hears… and loves you more than you can fathom.

He's listening.

From my broken heart filled with great hope,

Jill

Weeping may endure for a night, but
joy comes in the morning.

PSALM 30:5 (NKJV)

Surrender All

Creator and Keeper of all that exists, the world is Yours
and everything in it.
You have created all that we see and all that we don't.
You take care of everything.
Lord, You formed each of us in our mother's womb and
have created us for a purpose.
We are created in Your image.
You have fashioned us to bring You glory.

What does that all mean, God? Please show me.
How can I glorify You when I am hurting?
Do my tears honor You?
Is there purpose in my pain?
Help me to know You.
Help me to trust You and the everlasting promises You
have made.
Help me to believe You are good.
Please, Lord, help me to trust You with all that burdens
my heart right now.

I need Your help.
I need You.
I can't do this in my own strength.

Teach me and help me to remember that when I am
    weak, You are strong!
You will provide all I need to press on.
You will take care of everything that concerns me.
You are all that I need!
Help me to surrender.
My life is in Your hands.

> *Why are you downcast, O my soul? Why so*
> *disturbed within me? Put your hope in God, for*
> *I will yet praise him, my Savior and my God.*
>
> Psalm 42:11

In Your Hands

Heavenly Father, my life is in Your hands.
Yesterday, today, and forever, I am safe and secure in You.
Lord, please help me to know that You are in control.
Help me to believe You are at work in my life right now,
    even when I don't see it.
Help me to trust in what I do not see, when what I see
    is so painful.
Please help me to know You are taking care of my needs.

You are faithful and good, trustworthy and present.
In You I find grace and forgiveness, healing and hope.
You have not left me alone in my trials.
You are with me right now, and You have promised to
    never leave me nor forsake me.
Father, please help me to believe that Your plans for me
    and my family are good.

Lord, thank You for listening to my cries for help.
Thank You for loving me so much.

Help me to believe You and the promises You have
    made.
Forgive me when I doubt You and Your love.
I believe, Lord. Forgive me for my unbelief.

> *The LORD himself goes before you and will be
> with you; he will never leave you nor forsake
> you. Do not be afraid; do not be discouraged.*
>
> DEUTERONOMY 31:8

Trusting You Alone

You can be trusted completely, Lord.
When all else fails, You will never fail me.
You will never lie to me.
You will always keep Your promises.

Lord, if I have trusted in anything or anyone other than
    You, please forgive me and help me to seek You.
Lord, this world makes promises it cannot fulfill or
    keep.
You alone are the faithful Promise Keeper.

When I don't know where to turn, turn my heart
    toward You.
When I have exhausted all earthly options, help me to
    remember You.
When my eyes are filled with tears, lift my gaze toward
    heaven.
When I want to give up, cradle me in Your healing
    hands.

When it seems impossible to trust, please, Lord, do the
impossible in my heart.

Help me to trust You with my fears.
Help me to trust You with every tear.
Help me to trust You with my anger and frustration.
Lord, please help me to trust You with my doubt and
unbelief.
In every detail of my life, help me to trust You
completely.
In this very moment, I will trust You, Lord!

*Praise be to the LORD, for he has heard my cry for
mercy. The LORD is my strength and my shield; my
heart trusts in him, and I am helped. My heart
leaps for joy and I will give thanks to him in song.*

PSALM 28:6-7

Peace in the Midst of the Storm

In the midst of this storm, Jesus, You are the only One
who can bring peace.
You are the Prince of Peace.
Your peace surpasses all understanding.
Your peace guards my heart and mind.
You are my Peace.

Confusion and chaos demand my attention.
Fear and frustration invade my thoughts.
But You are all-knowing and all-powerful.
You can still the raging storm within me.
Your Word will quiet my heart and help me to breathe
again.

Where there is disorder, bring clarity.
Where there is anxiety, bring peace.
Help me to be still and know that You are God.

Please fill me with the assurance that You are in control.
Lord, please seal my heart and home with the
    unmistakable power of Your presence.
When I am full of despair, cover me in Your love.
When there is no reason to be at peace, be my Peace.
Lord, please bring me into Your peace so I can know
    You as my Prince of Peace.

*Do not be anxious about anything, but in everything,
by prayer and petition, with thanksgiving, present
your requests to God. And the peace of God,
which transcends all understanding, will guard
your hearts and your minds in Christ Jesus.*

PHILIPPIANS 4:6-7

Set Apart

Lord, Your Word says that before You formed me in
my mother's womb, You knew me, and before I was
born and inhaled my very first breath, You set me
apart.
When I was a child, did You prepare me for this?
Did You know that my heart would be crushed?
Did You set me apart to walk through this season of
sorrow?
I'm eager to know.

Did You see this coming and withhold Your hand?
When You planned this all out in eternity past, did You
know I would be crushed in spirit?
Did You know I would feel forsaken and ambushed by
fear?

Father, I'm desperate for You to do something,
anything to take this pain from me.
I'm weak and frail.

Every day I weep, crumpled in a heap of uncontrollable
anguish.

Is this the life I have been set apart for?
Please help me to understand what's going on.
And when I don't understand Your ways, help me to
just trust You.

Is this part of the good work You have prepared in
advance for me to do?
This can't be good, Lord.
But I don't want to retreat and run if this is where You
want me to be.
If this is where You are, then it's where I will stay.

In my heart I have set apart Christ as Lord, but right
now I feel so unprepared to give a reason for the
hope I have.

I'm a complete disaster.

Please deflate the self-centered arrogance in me that
would blind me from seeing the fullness of all You
have planned in my suffering.
Less of me, Lord Jesus, and more of You is what I long
for.

To You, my God, belong wisdom and power; counsel
and understanding.
To You belong all strength and victory.
What You tear down cannot be rebuilt. If You hold
back the waters, there is drought.
Lord, let Your living waters flow freely.
Rebuild what has been torn down within me.
Bring victory where I fear defeat.

*Know that the Lord has set apart the godly for
himself, the Lord will hear when I call to him.*

Psalm 4:3

Healing

Lord, You are the Healer.
You still heal today.
You heal hearts. You heal bodies.

Help us to believe that You still perform miracles in our
 day.
You are GOD!
You can do whatever You want, whenever You want to.
Nothing and no one can thwart Your plans.
Your purpose will always prevail. You are good, Lord.
Everything You do or don't do is right and true.

Lord, forgive me for doubting that You still heal people
 from sickness and diseases.
When the world says, "There is no cure," help me to
 remember You hold the cure.

When we are told, "There is no hope," help me to
 remember You are my hope.

23

When the shadow of death tries to consume me, You
are there.
You will never leave me. I am not alone in my pain.

When healing doesn't look as I thought it should, help
me to remember You created our inmost being and
know our every need.
When You choose not to heal this side of heaven, help
me to remember You know what You are doing.
I trust You.

Thank You that healing will come—in Your perfect
timing.
Lord, help me to continue to trust and wait for You.

*I am the LORD, the God of all mankind.
Is anything too hard for me?*

JEREMIAH 32:27

Out of Control

Lord, sometimes I feel as though everything around me
   is falling apart.

I feel so out of control—tired and useless.
I don't even have the energy to raise my head off my
   pillow each morning.
I'm scared, Lord.
I can't do this without You.
My mind and body need to rest.
I need rest for my heart and soul.
My insecurities, fears, and worries are ever before me.
I feel as though I'm drowning.

Please, Lord, come to my rescue!
Please do not withhold Your mercy from me.
I need You.

From the rising of the sun to the place where it sets—
   You are God.

In Your presence is fullness of joy, even in the midst of
    pain and trials.
Help me to rest in You.

I can't do this—but You can and You will.
Lord, You are the lifter of my head.
You are my strength.
You provide everything I need to survive.
You see me.
You know every struggle and every fear.
You are in control.

> *My grace is sufficient for you, for my*
> *power is made perfect in weakness.*
>
> 2 Corinthians 12:9

Everything Is Yours

When I look at my children, I am amazed.
You have blessed me beyond measure.
Lord, Your Word says that You knit them together in
    my womb.
I can't even imagine.

You know every detail about how my children are
    formed.
You determined the color of their eyes, the shape of
    their noses, and the intricacies of their innermost
    parts.
More than I know my children, You know them
    completely.
You were there when they were born.
And You will be there when they take their last breath.
You watch over their lives.

Jesus, You are the Alpha and the Omega,
The Beginning and the End of everything.

While You have entrusted them to me for a time, their
    times are in Your hands.
They belong to You.
You have numbered all of our days.
Lord, each breath that we take comes from You.
All that we have is Yours.

> *You created my inmost being; you knit me together
> in my mother's womb. I praise you because I am
> fearfully and wonderfully made; your works are
> wonderful, I know that full well. My frame was
> not hidden from you when I was made in the
> secret place. When I was woven together in the
> depths of the earth, your eyes saw my unformed
> body. All the days ordained for me were written
> in your book before one of them came to be.*
>
> PSALM 139:13-16

Fix My Focus

With all that's going on right now, it would be easy for me to focus on the trials at hand, but I don't want to do that.
When I focus on the circumstances, I take my eyes off You.

Lord, please help me to fix my eyes on You alone.
There is no possible way I can figure it all out.
No matter how hard I try to fix everything, I can't do it.
The more obsessed I am about making sense of it all, the more anxious and troubled my heart becomes.
I waste so much time trying to take matters into my own hands.
I overanalyze everything and ponder more than my mind can handle.
I feel out of control if I can't control the circumstances around me, even the people around me.

I'm exhausted.

Lord, free me from the need for answers.

Help me to surrender.

Jesus, You are the Good Shepherd.

In Your Name alone do I find everything I need and all
that I long for!

You hold the keys of life and the purpose of Your heart
prevails.

Creator of All—You have it all figured out.

Jesus, forgive me for trying to take on what only You
can handle.

Be my focus.

You are the answer.

It's all about You!

> *I will instruct you and teach you in the way you
> should go; I will counsel you and watch over you.*
>
> PSALM 32:8

Because You Know

Oh Lord, I'm so thankful I can come to You.
No matter what, You are always there for me.
I don't have to try and hide from You.
You know me.
You know my every thought.
Lord, You know my every need and desire.
I'm not afraid to share my deepest fears with You
    because You know.

You know my heart.

And right now, my heart is torn.
I have never felt such pain and sadness.
How long, Lord?
How long must I endure this heaviness of heart?
Carry me.
I've done all that I know to do.
I've prayed until I have no words left to pray.
I feel so helpless.

I don't understand why You continue to allow this
suffering.
Even if I did understand, it wouldn't take away the pain.
Oh Lord, You know the pain I'm talking about.
You know what it's like to suffer.
You know.

> *For I am the LORD, your God, who*
> *takes hold of your right hand and says*
> *to you, Do not fear; I will help you.*
>
> ISAIAH 41:13

In Need of Your Comfort

I need You.
Do You see me struggling?
The depths of who I am are overwhelmed.
I am crying out to You.
Do You hear me?

Lord, is there any other way?
I am weak, and my body and soul need rest.
Be my comfort.
Please bless me with Your peace and contentment.
In the midst of my struggles, fill me with Your healing
    Word.

Your Word is life to me.
It sustains and refreshes my soul.
Your truth sets me free!

Lord, this is so hard.
Please protect my life from peril and destruction.

I can't imagine life without You.
These trials increase my desire and longing for heaven,
    but You are the strength of my life.
When I am weak You are strong.

> *May your unfailing love be my comfort,*
> *according to your promise to your servant.*
>
> PSALM 119:76

Whatever Is True

So many things clamor for our attention, Lord.
Our focus and time are often spent on meaningless
things.
We search for what cannot satisfy and allow the junk of
this world to clutter our lives.

We are distracted.
Lord, be our focus.

Help me to be a living example of what it is to be Christ
centered.
Purify the areas in my life where I have allowed the
world in and the enemy access.
Please guide me into all truth so that all may see that
You are my life.
Whatever is true and noble, whatever is praiseworthy
and excellent, whatever is of You, Jesus, fix my heart
and mind on such things.

Lord, please protect my family and me from all that
    would try to distract us and draw us away from You.
When the temptations of this world entice us, please
    give us the strength to walk away.
Help us to know that Your way is best.
Help us always do the right thing because it's the right
    thing to do.
Please, heavenly Father, help us to be people after Your
    heart.
Encourage us with the truth of Your Word.
Pierce our hearts with an overwhelming affection for
    You.
You have all we need and desire.
You alone satisfy.

*Finally, brothers, whatever is true, whatever is
noble, whatever is right, whatever is pure, whatever
is lovely, whatever is admirable—if anything is
excellent or praiseworthy—think about such things.*

Philippians 4:8

Fear Not

Father, I'm afraid!
I'm overwhelmed!
Where are You?
I need YOU! I need You right now.

I feel empty, confused, and scared.
I can't think straight.
My life is full of disorder and chaos.
Ungodly thoughts and fears torment me day and night.

I am not at peace right now.
I need Your help just to breathe.
Please free me from this moment.
I need to escape. I want to run away!

Protect me from myself, Lord.
You have promised to never leave me.
Your perfect love casts out all my fears.
I can "fear not," for You are with me.

"God has not given us a spirit of fear, but of power and
    of love and of a sound mind" (2 Timothy 1:7 NKJV).

I am not alone in this battle being waged against me.
The battle is Yours.
The chains of fear are gone; You have set me free.
Lord, I believe!
Please forgive me for my unbelief!

> *I call to God, and the LORD saves me.*
> *Evening, morning and noon I cry out*
> *in distress, and he hears my voice.*
>
> PSALM 55:16-17

What Only You Can Do

Lord, I expect too much from people.
The expectations I have of others can only be met in
    You.
You alone can satisfy every craving I have.
You alone can fill the emptiness in my soul.

Lord, I am so needy.
I have looked to this world for answers and have come
    up empty.
I have trusted in people who have let me down again
    and again.
Father, forgive me for expecting others to do what only
    You can do.
Help me to let people off the hook.
Please help me to cast all my cares upon You, Lord, for
    You care for me.
When I am struggling, worried, and stressed, please
    guide me into all truth.

I can't change others.

I can't change my circumstances.

I can't even change myself—but You can.

Teach me Your ways, Father, and help me to walk in humility.

"May the words of my mouth and the meditation of my heart be pleasing in your sight,

O Lord, my Rock and my Redeemer" (Psalm 19:14).

Keep me from being distracted by many things.

Open my heart and mind to all that You would have for me today.

Heavenly Father, You will not disappoint me.

You are faithful, and I can trust You completely.

It is better to take refuge in the
Lord than to trust in man.

Psalm 118:8

My Purpose

Lord, I have so many roles to play.
Wife, mother, daughter, friend—the list goes on.
I'm lacking in all areas.
I can't please everyone all the time.
I feel stretched beyond my limit, and I'm tired.
I can't live like this.

Father, this road is long and hard.
Would You please intervene?
In every area of my life, please rescue me!
I can't live without You.
Teach me Your ways, Lord, so I can walk in truth.
Show me who I am in You.
Why am I so hard on myself? I'm not perfect.
Free me from the burdens I'm not meant to carry.

Lord, thank You for being my Father.
Thank You for putting up with me and loving me no
    matter what.
You are so patient.

Help me to be content in whatever circumstance I find
myself.

Help me to draw strength from You every day.

You are aware of everything that's going on, and You'll
take care of it.

Lord, please bless me with eyes to see the multitude of
blessings all around me.

The greatest privilege I have in this life is being Your
child.

You know me and created me for a purpose that You
will faithfully fulfill.

Thank You, Lord.

> *Though I walk in the midst of trouble, you preserve*
> *my life…The LORD will fulfill [his purpose]*
> *for me; your love, O LORD, endures forever.*
>
> PSALM 138:7-8

Brokenness Made Whole

Why can't everything work out?
Why does life have to be like this?
Why must we endure painful trials and temptations?

I want life to be different.
I don't want to suffer, and I don't want my loved ones to
    suffer.
I don't want a superficial marriage full of selfishness
    and strife.
I'm so tired of bad news, death, and destruction. War
    and conflict are everywhere.
There is no escape. This world is broken.
I am broken.

But You, O Lord, have come to heal the brokenhearted.
You have come to bind up our wounds.
You have come to strengthen the weak and guide the
    wayward.

Jesus, You defeated death on the cross so that life won't
always be like this.

Because of Your great love, we can know true and
lasting LOVE.

You were broken for me so that in my brokenness I can
run to You.

Because of Your suffering, someday there will be no
more pain and no more tears.

We can bring our broken hearts and open wounds to
You because You are greater than all this world has
to offer.

We can surrender our desires to You, Lord, for You are
greater than our hearts and You know everything.

Thank You for allowing me to pour out my frustrations
and fears before You.

You understand me.

Thank You, Jesus, for taking the broken pieces of my
life to form a tapestry of glory.

Only You can do the impossible.

He gives strength to the weary and
increases the power of the weak.

Isaiah 40:29

Be Near

Where are You, Lord?
Why do You seem so far away?
We draw near to You, Lord.
We have nowhere else to go.
Please draw near, Father.
How long will You wait, Lord?
How long will You wait to free us?

Please bring healing, Lord.
You are the Great Physician.
You know what man cannot figure out.
You know all things.

You have created everything we need for life and
    godliness.
You are the Author of life.
There is nothing that surprises You or throws You off.
You know exactly what we need right now.

Be involved in the intimate details of our health and
healing.
Please give us wisdom and direction.
You are not surprised by the painful trials we are
walking through right now.
You love us infinitely.
Thank You for drawing near to us in our time of great
need.
We will never walk alone.

*Look to the L*ORD *and his strength;*
seek his face always.

PSALM 105:4

When I Don't Understand

I don't understand why all of this is happening.
I can't fight this battle.
I hate suffering.
I cannot bear to walk through this one more day, one
    more hour, one more minute.
My hearts aches!

We need You now, Lord.
How long, God?
Please do something!
We are desperate for You.
Please intervene!
Strengthen us for this journey.
We cannot endure without You.

Please reveal Yourself right now, Lord.
Perform a miracle in our day.
Show us that You are in the midst of all that is going on
    and that You care.

Please, Lord, bring healing, hope, and restoration.

Reach down, Father, and rescue us.

Thank You, Lord, for life!

Even in the midst of this season of heartbreak, every day is a gift.

Help me to trust You.

Help me to trust You when I don't understand Your ways.

Please help me to trust You in everything.

> *I lift up my eyes to the hills—where does my help come from? My help comes from the LORD, the Maker of heaven and earth.*
>
> PSALM 121:1-2

It's Okay to Cry

Lord, You see my tears.
Help me to remember that it's okay to cry.
I don't always have to be strong.
I don't have to hide my pain from You.
Sometimes I just want to cry.
Sometimes I can't stop crying.

Thank You for tears.
Thank You for giving us a way to express our deepest
    emotions.
I don't know what I would do if I couldn't release the
    pain in my heart.
Your Word says that You collect our tears in a bottle.
Thank You, Lord.

It brings me great comfort to know You care about me.
You care enough about my pain to gather my tears.
Although I must admit it seems impossible, You are the
    God of the impossible.

You said it and I choose to believe it.
Thank You, Lord, for allowing me to pour out my heart
   before You.
You can be trusted.
Not a single tear is wasted.
Thank You, Lord.

> *You keep track of all my sorrows. You have*
> *collected all my tears in your bottle. You*
> *have recorded each one in your book.*
>
> PSALM 56:8 (NLT)

Thank You, Lord

It seems as though when I should praise You and thank You for the countless blessings You have given me, I question and doubt Your goodness.

Oh Lord, forgive me.

You are so patient and kind.

Thank You for my family: _____

_____ .

Thank You for revealing Yourself to us through Your Word.

Lord, please continue to hide Your Word in our hearts.

Thank You for helping us to persevere when we want to give up.

Thank You for allowing us to experience pain and suffering so that we recognize our need for You.

Thank You for delivering us from the enemy's snare.

Lord, You are all-powerful. Our hope is in You.

Thank You, Lord, for commanding Your angels to watch over and protect us.

We are safe in Your care. Thank You for turning our
hearts toward You.

Keep us heavenly minded and earthly good.

Lord, when we are tempted to complain, help us to
remember all You have done.

Help us to remember You.

You have saved us and set us free.

You have set eternity in our hearts

And given us hope beyond this life.

We have so much to look forward to.

Because of Your love and grace, we can face another day,
another trial, another disappointment.

Thank You for giving us more of Yourself, even when
we don't deserve You.

*Be joyful always; pray continually; give
thanks in all circumstances, for this is
God's will for you in Christ Jesus.*

1 Thessalonians 5:16-18

Joy No Matter What

Lord, You alone are the Author of real joy.
We can have joy in the midst of the mundane.
We can have joy in the midst of deep pain.
When everything around us falls apart, we can still
     have joy.

Sounds good, but is it real?
Is it possible to have joy no matter what?

When tears keep flowing and seem to have no end, is it
     really possible to have joy?
When dreams are devastated and all hope lost, can joy
     be found?
When our world has been shattered, can we be joyful?

Without You, Lord, it's impossible.
Joy doesn't exist apart from You.
So when everything falls apart and all worldly hope is
     gone, You are still God and You are there.

In this life we will have trials, but You are the source of
joy in the midst of them.
There is no greater joy than knowing You.
You are the real joy we seek.
You are the joy in the midst of our sorrows.
You are the joy that encourages us to press on another
day.

Thank You for releasing us from the burden of seeking
joy in all the wrong places.
Thank You for rescuing us from the longing to find
happiness in worldly things.
Forgive us for desiring anything more than You.
Lord, in You we find fullness of joy!

Those who sow in tears will reap with songs of joy.
PSALM 126:5

Nothing Compares

Gracious Father, sometimes life is so hard.
The everyday stuff on top of new struggles makes some
 days unbearable.
Help me to look to You for strength.
When I am weak, please make me strong.
Let no weapon formed against my family and me
 prosper.

I don't know what's going to happen, and it scares me
 to think about it.
But I believe You are in control.
I give it all to You.
I lay my burdens at Your feet and trust You with the
 outcome.
I seek the rest, peace, and joy only You can give.
You are my refuge.
You shelter me from the raging storms of life and guide
 me to safety.

Lord, help me to be grateful and give You thanks in all
    circumstances.
Please cleanse me from the sin that tries to entangle me.
Shine Your light into any area of darkness in my life.
Breathe Your life into me.
Refresh my soul, Jesus.
My life is in Your hands.
Nothing compares to You.

> *Keep me safe, O God, for in you I take
> refuge. I said to the LORD, "You are my Lord;
> apart from you I have no good thing."*
>
> PSALM 16:1-2

One More Day

Lord, thank You for today.
Even after a sleepless night, I'm thankful for another
    day.
Although nothing has changed, I thank You for today.
Even as I sit here and ponder the many challenges and
    obstacles our family will face, I'm so thankful that
    You have given us one more day.

Today is a gift from You. Help us to rejoice and be glad
    in it.
You know every detail of what this day holds.
Father, please wrap me in Your love and help me to
    press on.
Give me the courage and confidence I need to live for
    You today.
Your love is deeper and more intense than I can
    comprehend.
I can't fathom that kind of love.

Help me to know I am beautiful in Your sight.

Please reveal Yourself to me today in a way only You can.

Lord, help me to fear not, for You are with me always.

Please help me to find comfort in You and shield me from all that would try to harm me today.

Please fill me with peace that surpasses all understanding.

Open my eyes so I can see You in the midst of this darkness.

Lord, please give me the wisdom and divine guidance I need to be who You created me to be today.

I long to trust You completely with all that I am and all that I have.

Help me to trust You.

Every day is one day closer to seeing You face-to-face, Jesus.

Until that day, help me to press on.

He will call upon me, and I will answer
him; I will be with him in trouble, I
will deliver him and honor him.

PSALM 91:15

Too Much

Creator God, Ruler, Maker, and Keeper—stretch out
Your hand and save us.
Hear the unspoken urgency in our hearts.
We need You.
This is too much for our family to bear.
We are exhausted.
We are weak.
We don't know what to do.
Where else can we go?

You have given us more than we can handle, but You
have not left us alone.
Heavenly Father, Your grace is sufficient in our
weakness.
You are closer than our very breath.
Help us to not lean on our own understanding but trust
and acknowledge You in everything.
We were never meant to walk alone.
We have You.

You are all we need.
You are God.
No one and nothing compares to You.

> *In my anguish I cried to the LORD, and he*
> *answered by setting me free. The LORD is with*
> *me; I will not be afraid. What can man do to*
> *me? The LORD is with me; he is my helper.*

PSALM 118:5-7

Where Are You?

I know You see my brokenness.
You see my bleeding heart.
Why are You silent?
Why do You seem so distant right now?
"Do not be far from me, for trouble is near and there is
    no one to help" (Psalm 22:11).
Where are You?

Sometimes it seems as though when I need You most,
    You are nowhere to be found.
Have I lost my way?
Why can't I see You at work in my anguish?
Is there a veil over my eyes?
"Hear my cry, O God; listen to my prayer. From the
    ends of the earth I call to you, I call as my heart
    grows faint; lead me to the rock that is higher than
    I. For you have been my refuge, and a strong tower"
    (Psalm 61:1-3).
You are my hope and my deliverance.

You are greater than my heart, and You know everything.

Though my mind, heart, and flesh may fail me and tempt me to doubt You, You are the strength of my life and my portion forever.

In the midst of this darkness, please give me clarity of mind.

Please help me to trust You even when I can't see You or sense that You are with me.

Lord, sear my heart with this truth: "The LORD himself goes before you and will be with you; he will never leave you nor forsake you. Do not be afraid; do not be discouraged" (Deuteronomy 31:8).

I'm so thankful that no matter what tricks my mind may play on me, Your Word is true. You will never leave me.

Even though I walk through the valley of the shadow of death, where the pieces of my heart are scattered about, and even though You seem so far away right now...I will not fear.

I will not fear the enemy and all his evil torments or the lies he throws my way, for You are with me. Your rod and Your staff comfort me.

My hope is in You.

I have chosen you and have not rejected you. So do not fear, for I am with you; do not be dismayed, for I am your God. I will strengthen you and help you; I will uphold you with my righteous right hand.

Isaiah 41:9-10

In My Struggles

Something good will come of this, I just know it.
I trust You, Lord.
You have begun a good work in me You have promised
    to complete.
If my present struggles and heartbreak are part of what
    You are doing, I will trust You.
I will continue to hope and believe I will see Your
    goodness even now…through all the tears.

Keep me from focusing so much on my pain that I
    forget You.
Keep me from being self-absorbed.
Help me to embrace You even though I don't
    understand why You have allowed this to happen.
Help me to stop doubting You.
When I don't understand Your ways, please increase my
    faith.
Help me to be sure of what I hope for and certain of
    what I do not see.

But I am weary, Lord.

When I want to fall under the weight of this burden, lift me out of the mud and mire of my afflictions and set my feet on a rock.

Please give me a firm place to stand.

Oh Lord, put a new song in my mouth, a hymn of praise to You.

Let my struggles be a witness to all that You are God and there is no other.

Let those who peer into the midst of this chaos see that You are a faithful and mighty God. That You are full of love and compassion.

Holy Spirit, help me in my weakness.

Thank You for interceding for me when I can't even find the words to pray.

In my anguish, I cry out to You…and You answer by setting me free.

You are with me. I will not be afraid.

I will rejoice in the midst of my struggles because You are my helper.

I can't even imagine trying to endure these trials without You.

Thank You, God, that I don't have to.

Though I walk in the midst of trouble, you preserve my life; you stretch out your hand against the anger of my foes, with your right hand you save me. The LORD will fulfill [his purpose] for me; your love, O LORD, endures forever—do not abandon the works of your hands.

PSALM 138:7-8

Change Us

Lord, You have allowed our family to see and
experience deep pain and suffering.
As a result of the journey we are on, allow us to become
the people You desire us to be.
Keep bitterness and hatred far from us.
Protect us from hardness of heart and self-pity.
Give us the freedom to express our fears.

Please, Lord, help us to persevere and walk in humility.
Teach us to be thankful no matter what, and bless us
with a deep desire to please You.
Lord, change us from the inside out.
As a result of the work You have begun in our hearts, I
pray our lives would reflect Your light and truth.
We don't have to try harder, Lord. We just need to trust
You to finish the work You have started.

Help our family to be an example of what it looks like
to have real joy in the midst of deep heartache.

And Lord, allow us to extend the comfort we have received from You to others.

Praise be to the God and Father of our Lord Jesus Christ, the Father of compassion and the God of all comfort, who comforts us in all our troubles, so that we can comfort those in any trouble with the comfort we ourselves have received from God.

2 Corinthians 1:3-4

Come to My Rescue

In my brokenness You will make me whole.
You alone can take the shattered fragments of my heart
    and mend them back together.
Every piece of my life that has brought me to this place
    of complete desperation has not gone unnoticed by
    You.
Where I am right now is no surprise to You.
You see me.
You know.

Please strengthen me, Lord.
Be the lifter of my head and the rock on which I stand.
Show me the way out of this place.
Draw me into Your loving embrace.
Lead me to the well where I may drink deeply from
    Your life.
Come to my rescue and quench my parched and weary
    soul.

While I wait for You, please keep my heart from
growing cold.

Help me to trust in Your perfect plan and purpose for
my pain.

My brokenness is beautiful to You because You make
all things new.

Your purpose will prevail, though the plans in my heart
are many.

I need You.

If this brokenness will allow me to see You more clearly,
Lord, then I'm all Yours.

Open my eyes so that I might see a glimpse of what You
are doing even now.

> *The LORD is close to the brokenhearted and*
> *saves those who are crushed in spirit.*
>
> PSALM 34:18

Will You Fight for Me?

Come quickly, Lord, and rescue me.
Save me from this anguish that threatens to overcome
    me.
I can't seem to focus on anything but the pain.
Sorrow continues to envelop my mind and heart.
I am distracted and distraught.
I am entangled by hopelessness and fear.
The unknown scares me to death.

Will I make it through?
Will You deliver me once again?
Will You fight for me?

Please be gracious to me, Lord.
Be my strength and my hope.
Spread Your mighty protection over me and pour out
    Your favor upon my life.

Even when all hope seems lost, Your promises remain.

You give strength to the weary.
You rescue the wayward.
You mend the broken and heal the sick.
You are God.
There is none like You.

> *I am the LORD, your God, who takes*
> *hold of your right hand and says to*
> *you, Do not fear; I will help you.*
>
> ISAIAH 41:13

My Strength
and My Song

God, You are amazing.
Your grace and mercy reach beyond my comprehension.
Your love is far greater than anything I can imagine.

Thank You for another day to live for You.
Thank You for another day to love.
There is no end to Your goodness and faithfulness.
Thank You for all that You have done and continue to
    do in my life.

You are my strength and my song.
Jesus, thank You for loving me enough to give Your life
    for me so that I might live.
My life is not worth living without You.
My heart's desire is to know You.

And yet my heart is so frail.
My faith is so weak.

My strength is gone.
My doubt gets the best of me.
But You love me anyway.

You are faithful, when I am not.
You forgive and You forget.
You restore and renew.
Jesus, You are my all in all.
You are the strength of my life.

> *God is our refuge and strength, an*
> *ever-present help in trouble.*
>
> Psalm 46:1

I Am Yours

"Search me, O God, and know my heart; test me
and know my anxious thoughts. See if there is
any offensive way in me, and lead me in the way
everlasting" (Psalm 139:23-24).
My life is in Your hands.
You give me every breath.
You are life to me.
Take all that I am in this moment and help me to
surrender.

I'm a mess.
I'm undone.
But I am Yours.
Forever.

You are working all this out for good.
You will take the ashes of my life and make them
beautiful.

You will finish the work You have started in my life
    because I am Yours.
Nothing and no one can take Your love from me.
You love me eternally and infinitely right now.

Lord, I long to be pure before You.
Rescue me from the grip of self-pity and self-
    righteousness.
Cleanse me for Your glory and praise.
I long to be fully Yours.
Take all that I am.

I am Yours.

> *I have summoned you by name; you are mine...I
> will be with you...Since you are precious and
> honored in my sight, and because I love you.*
> ISAIAH 43:1-2,4

You Are Life to Me

There's nothing I can do about yesterday.
I can't go back.
I can't have a do over.
Yesterday is gone.
But today is a new day.
Today is right now.
And the future is in Your loving, secure hands.

You are the same yesterday, today, and forever.
Though everything around me continues to change,
    You remain.
You are constant.
You will never change.

You are the Maker of all that exists.
You are the Healer of the nations.
You are the Comforter of my heart and the Keeper of
    my soul.
You are my Savior and Redeemer.

In this sea of pain, You will protect me from the torrent
of heartbreak crashing down on me.
Your heart is full of compassion and Your love never
fails.
I can depend on You.
I can hope in You.
I can live.

*See, I am doing a new thing! Now it springs
up; do you not perceive it? I am making a way
in the desert and streams in the wasteland.*

Isaiah 43:19

When I Question and Doubt

Who am I that I should question You?
"'For my thoughts are not your thoughts, neither are
    your ways my ways,' declares the LORD. 'As the
    heavens are higher than the earth, so are my ways
    higher than your ways and my thoughts than your
    thoughts'" (Isaiah 55:8).
But my mind is racing with questions and pierced with
    doubt.
My heart is full of sorrow.
And I long to know why this has happened.

I can't live like this, Lord.
I don't think I can endure this trial any longer.
This burden is dreadfully heavy.
Did You turn away when I needed You?
When will this onslaught of doubt disappear?
How long will You wait to lift this?

Until You do, I will rest in You.

I will rest in Your love and grace.
I will hide in the shadow of Your perfect peace.
I will trust in the providence of Your presence.
I will dive into the depths of Your love.

> *My soul finds rest in God alone; my salvation*
> *comes from him. He alone is my rock and my*
> *salvation; he is my fortress, I will never be shaken.*
>
> PSALM 62:1

I Feel Empty

This pain is more than I can bear.
It's as if I'm dwindling away as each day goes by.
I go through the motions of life, and yet I feel nothing.
I feel absolutely numb.
I feel empty.

My heart continues to beat, yet I'm so dead inside.
I long to wake up from this living nightmare.
Is this it?
Is this the depths to which a broken heart can take you?
Will this be my life?

I look around and see people smiling and laughing,
    enjoying the simple things in life.
Will I ever experience happiness again?
Will I ever stop pretending and truly enjoy this life?
Will I?
Is it even possible?

Lord, in this moment I choose to fix my eyes "not on
what is seen, but on what is unseen. For what is
seen is temporary, but what is unseen is eternal"
(2 Corinthians 4:18).

Even when You seem so far away, Your Word says that
You "are close to the brokenhearted" and You save
"those who are crushed in spirit" (Psalm 34:18).
Therefore, I will trust in You and know that You will
rescue me.
You are the Lord, the God of all mankind.

You are the fullness I need in this empty place.
You have formed me and know the intimate details of
who I am.
You will not leave me broken.
You will carry me and sustain me.
You will take Your mighty, loving hands and securely
hold the pieces of my life.

You will fill me to overflowing.
You will accomplish in my heart and life more than I
can imagine.
You will mend and make new.
You will.

Listen to me...you whom I have upheld since you were conceived, and have carried since your birth. Even to your old age and gray hairs I am he, I am he who will sustain you. I have made you and will carry you; I will sustain you and will rescue you.

ISAIAH 46:3-4

I Need You

Father, please help me.
Take hold of me.
Open my eyes so that I might see beyond my
    circumstances.
Help me to see with Your eyes the tapestry of life You
    are weaving all around me.
You are life to me.

I need You.
"Before a word is on my tongue, you know it completely,
    O Lord" (Psalm 139:4).
You know my every thought.
You see every tear.
You hear me when I cry.

Though life continues to come crashing down all
    around me, and joy is nowhere in sight, though the
    mountains be shaken and the hills be removed, yet

Your unfailing love for me will not be shaken and
Your covenant of peace will not be removed.
"You will keep in perfect peace him whose mind is
steadfast, because he trusts in You" (Isaiah 26:3).
I trust You, Lord.

Fill my emptiness with Your love and presence.
Please keep me from all harm and watch over my life.
Replace this barrenness with the truth of who You are.
You are my joy.
You are life to me.

*The LORD will keep you from all harm—he will
watch over your life; the LORD will watch over
your coming and going both now and forevermore.*

PSALM 121:7-8

You Left Your Heart with Me

You came to me and touched me and I'll never be the
 same.
I'm overwhelmed.
This is incredible, even indescribable.
The person I was has died and I am a new person, a new
 creation in You.

You promised that You are coming back again, coming
 to take me away and dry my tears.
To keep me safe with You forever.

Until then, You have left Your heart with me.
And it breaks with the things that break You and it
 rejoices with the things You rejoice in, because I feel
 what You feel.
I love with Your love.

You have left Your heart with me so I can know You
and Your hopes, Your Word, and Your plan.

I've been born again. I am Your child.
I will cry out to You…Abba, Father…Daddy.
Please, Daddy, come quickly.
And I will follow the still, small voice I hear as Your
heart whispers to mine…
"I'm here, child. I'm here with you."

Because you are sons, God sent the Spirit
of his Son into our hearts, the Spirit
who calls out, "Abba, Father."

GALATIANS 4:6

The Cross

Why won't turning over a new leaf bring new life?
Why must I live in resurrection life, life that has passed
through death?
Lord, You set the conditions of discipleship: "If anyone
would come after me, he must deny himself and
take up his cross and follow me" (Matthew 16:24).

Is this my cross to carry?
Is this heart-wrenching experience the thorn in my
flesh that will not be removed?
Is this a time when Your grace must be sufficient in my
life?

The cross isn't the harmless glittering decoration we
have made it out to be.
It wounds; it destroys. And yet it also brings life.
Lord, You know this, and You call us to die on it that
we might live in You forever.

The cross is not for cowards.
Because you can't pretend to love unless you live a lie.
You can't pretend that loving people will never hurt.
It hurts deeply.

Oh Lord, I am nothing without You.
I need to drink from Your living waters.
I want to hear, "Well done, My good and faithful
    servant!"
And I know I must feel the weight of the beam before I
    feel the joy of Your words.
I must wear a crown of thorns before I wear a crown of
    glory.
Lord, I long to love You that much.
Help me to love You enough to die to myself.

> *I have been crucified with Christ and I no
> longer live, but Christ lives in me. The life I
> live in the body, I live by faith in the Son of
> God, who loved me and gave himself for me.*
>
> GALATIANS 2:20

In Repentance and Returning

I know You are my Father. I know You are always with
  me.
But trials are everywhere I turn, tempting me to deny
  Your love and mocking my faith in You.

Yet even when my faith falters, You are always faithful.
And when I fall, You tenderly wrap Your arms around
  me and help me back up again.
Your grace empowers me always.

In repentance and returning I find rest.
I find that hardship and suffering drive me closer to
  You…to my knees where I always find You.
There's always a way through where all things become
  new.

I am comforted with the comfort You have given me.
I can then weep with those who weep and shine for
  those in darkness.

For You meet me where I am and catch each falling tear.
You redeem each wasted year and soothe each raging
fear.

So I glory in my weakness, and I trust in Your strength.
Though burned by fiery trials, in repentance and
returning I find rest.

This is what the Sovereign Lord, the Holy One
of Israel, says: "In repentance and rest is your
salvation, in quietness and trust is your strength."
ISAIAH 30:15

Scars

Lord, this pain will certainly leave a scar.
Had I not loved so deeply, certainly the mark of
    heartbreak would be long gone by now.
But still I thank You for the privilege of loving so deeply.
Thank You for loving me first.
I know what love is because You gave so much.
You gave Your life away for me—for my life, my joy, my
    eternity—for my scars.

Will You take everything I have surrendered into Your
    hands and make it Yours?
Will You be glorified through this shattered vessel?
Will You spread Your love over all this hurt?
Will You make my scars beautiful?

My tears are Yours, for to You alone I lift up my life.
You are my Healer.
You are a whisper of hope.
When the troubles of this moment try to block out all

that is life, You break through the darkness and lead me to safety.

These trials that seem to never end—they will end someday.
You are my promise of life.
In Your love I find redemption.
In Your Word I find life.
Jesus, because of Your scars I can run to You with mine.
I hold on to You always, Lord, because You are enough.

He himself bore our sins in his body on the
tree, so that we might die to sins and live for
righteousness; by his wounds you have been healed.
1 PETER 2:24

At All Times

You are God.
From everlasting to everlasting Your sovereign hand
rules the earth.
The mountain peaks bow down to You alone.
The waves of the sea halt to Your voice.
The sun rises and sets because You say so.

"Ah, Sovereign LORD, you have made the heavens and
the earth by your great power and outstretched
arm. Nothing is too hard for you...Great are your
purposes and mighty are your deeds. Your eyes are
open to all the ways of men" (Jeremiah 32:17,19).
At all times You are watching over my life.
Because of Your greatness, "I will meditate on all your
works and consider all your mighty deeds" (Psalm
77:12).
At all times You are able to do immeasurably more than
I can ask or imagine.

You see me and know the depth of my need.

Because of Your great love, I am not consumed, for
Your compassions never fail. "They are new every
morning; great is your faithfulness. I say to myself,
'The LORD is my portion therefore I will wait for
him' " (Lamentations 3:23-24).

Lord, keep me anchored to Your relentless love.
As I come before Your throne with the cries of my torn
heart, hear me.
At all times, let the words from my mouth and the
meditations of my heart please You.

My soul sings, though my heart aches.
My hands are raised to heaven, though my head is
bowed low.
Tears stream down my cheeks as I cling to You, my
Strength.
"Because your love is better than life, my lips will glorify
you" (Psalm 63:3).

My life and times are in Your merciful, mighty hands.
Your Word stands forever.
"There is no wisdom, no insight, no plan that can
succeed against the LORD" (Proverbs 21:30).

You alone are God.
At all times You are for me.

> *Trust in him at all times, O people; pour out*
> *your hearts to him, for God is our refuge.*
>
> PSALM 62:8

To Know You More

Lord, I long to know You more intimately.
Please draw me into where You can be found.
Please direct my heart into Your love and Christ's
perseverance.
My mind is scattered, and these trials have caused me
to feel tattered and torn.

Oh Lord, I pray that out of Your glorious riches You
would strengthen me with power through Your
Spirit in my inner being, so that Christ may dwell
in my heart through faith. And I pray that being
rooted and established in love, I may have power,
together with all the saints, to grasp how wide and
long and high and deep is the love of Christ and to
know this love that surpasses knowledge that I may
be filled to the measure of all the fullness of God.

You know where all the hurt is buried.

Please break up the hardened surface of my heart and
release me.
Penetrate the festering wounds that keep me from
being vulnerable and willing.
Lord, let this be a time of refreshing.
Though I feel so ragged and messy, please keep away all
that would hinder me from drawing near to You.
The craziness I find myself in is trying to steal my peace.
Protect me, Lord.

I want to come out of this season knowing You more.
Loving You more.
I pray that not a tear would be wasted. Those who have
long been withheld I release into Your care.
I trust You to use every moment during this time of
despair.

Hold my heart, Lord.
Please reveal Yourself to me.
I need to fellowship with You in my suffering.
You know how I feel.
My soul yearns, even faints for You, Lord. "My heart
and flesh cry out for the Living God" (Psalm 84:2).
You are the abundance that I lack.
Oh Lord, I long to know You more.

*I want to know Christ and the power of his
resurrection and the fellowship of sharing in his
sufferings, becoming like him in his death, and so,
somehow, to attain to the resurrection from the dead.*

PHILIPPIANS 3:10

Proved Genuine

Is this faith of mine for real? Or will I fall under the
weight of my doubt? Will I be found a faithful
follower when all is said and done? Or will I crack
under this mantle of suffering? Will this pain stifle
me and keep me silent?

Lord, I want to be fully Yours.

In Your great mercy You have given me new birth into
a living hope through the resurrection from the
dead of Your precious Son, Jesus Christ, and into an
inheritance that can never perish, spoil, or fade—
kept in heaven for me, because through faith I am
shielded by Your great power until the coming
salvation that is ready to be revealed in the last time.

In this I long to greatly rejoice, Lord, though now for a
little while I have had to suffer grief in all kinds of
trials. You have said that these have come into my

life at this time so that my faith—of greater worth than gold, which perishes even though refined by fire—may be proved genuine and may result in praise, glory, and honor when Jesus Christ is revealed.

Jesus, though I have not seen You, I love You...I love You so much; and even though I do not see You now, in the midst of these trials, I still believe You, and I am filled to overflowing with an inexpressible and glorious joy, for I am receiving the goal of my faith, the salvation of my soul.

Therefore, Lord Jesus, please prepare my mind for action. Help me to be self-controlled. Set my hope fully on the grace to be given to me when You are revealed.

Please keep me from conforming to the evil desires I once had when I lived in ignorance, apart from You. Keep me from falling back into my youthful, naive ways. And, Lord, help me to be holy, because You are holy.

Jesus, if in these tribulations my faith is being proved genuine, then I'm thankful.

I praise You for allowing me to go through this,
     knowing that You have not left me alone.
As tears stain my pillows and moisten my cheeks, You
     are here.
You know my heart.
My faith is in Your hands.
As You hold me, You hold and protect the measure of
     faith that You, Yourself, have given me.
Thank You, Jesus!

*Without faith it is impossible to please God, because
anyone who comes to him must believe that he exists
and that he rewards those who earnestly seek him.*

Hebrews 11:6

(A portion of this prayer is taken from 1 Peter 1:1-16.)

When Prayers Aren't Answered

I've knocked and knocked, and still the door stays
    closed.
I've cried and cried till my tears run dry...heart broken,
    hopes dashed, dreams crushed.
The doubts insist on rearing their ugly heads, but I don't
    doubt You, Lord.
I don't doubt Your love or Your promises.

I question my heart and second-guess my motives,
    wondering if I hunger and thirst for righteousness...
    or am I just too tired to fight this fight anymore?
Do I over-spiritualize my longings, hoping to please
    You, hoping to persuade You to answer according to
    my will rather than Yours?

You are silent, and I am sad and confused...until a soft,
    soothing whisper fills my heart and echoes through

my soul, strengthening me as I realize You are the
Lord and I love Your will.

I long for it.

I discover that there are worse things than when prayers
aren't answered.
Such as when prayers aren't prayed, and they just wither
unsaid in the heart.
There is no joy like falling at Your feet and watching
You capture my tears…when my prayers are prayed.

> *Be joyful always; pray continually; give
> thanks in all circumstances, for this is
> God's will for you in Christ Jesus.*
>
> 1 THESSALONIANS 5:16-18

In Your Grip

Nothing can pry me from Your grip.
No one can tear me from Your love.
Yours aren't promises just made; they are promises kept.
Even to my last breath and on into eternity.

And You stay with me, to keep me true and close to You.
Even when I turn my back on You, You never turn Your
    back on me.

If You are for me, who can be against me?
What can separate me from Your love?
What force can challenge Your love?
Death tried but couldn't hold You.
Evil tried and failed.
Nothing can tear me from Your grip.
What confidence I have as I walk through this life,
    knowing I am Yours.

In his hand is the life of every creature
and the breath of all mankind.

JOB 12:10

Daddy

So many names for so many things.

You placed the stars in the sky and call them out by name.

Even the billions of stars that paint the night sky have names.

Amazing.

So many names for You, Lord.

You are my Peace, the Mighty God, the Everlasting One, my Provider, my Hope, the Bread of Life, Living Water, Love, my Comforter, my Counselor, the Way, the Truth, the Life.

So many names to bless my soul.

So many names to encourage me and give me confidence.

I am in awe, and I love them all.

But the name I love the most is the one Jesus used over and over.

Was it His favorite too?

Abba, Father…
Daddy…

You are my Daddy.
You are where I run.
Into Your loving embrace I hide.
Now, more than ever, I need You to be my Daddy.
I need You to whisper Your love over me.
I need to hear You say, "I love you."
As Your child, I long to find all that I need in You alone.
Take care of me, Daddy.
I need You.

> *For you did not receive a spirit that makes you a*
> *slave again to fear, but you received the Spirit of*
> *sonship. And by him we cry, "Abba, Father."*
>
> ROMANS 8:15

Before I Knew You

I was lost and alone before You came to me.
I was full of shame until You set me free.
I was selfish, stubborn, and shallow before I knew You.
I was blind and could not see all that You had given me.
I was lost and afraid.
I was restless and lonely.
Before You rescued me I was wrapped up in a life of
    destruction and despair.

But then You came and You gave.
You gave Your precious life away and saved me.
My sin, my life apart from You, was nailed on that cross.
You were pierced for my transgressions and crushed for
    my iniquities, and the punishment that I deserved,
    that brought me peace, was upon You, my Jesus.

Because of You, I am saved.
Because of Your suffering, Your wounds, I am healed!
I am free!

You did it all…

For me.

Not because I deserved it, and not because I was worthy, but because of Your great love.

Because of Your perfection and the purposes in Your heart.

You are amazing.

Alleluia.

Thank You, Lord.

Thank You for all You have done to give me abundant life even in the midst of a broken world.

Thank You for helping me to see my trials in light of all that You have done.

Thank You for knowing me and loving me before I ever knew You.

> *God demonstrates his own love for us in this:*
> *While we were still sinners, Christ died for us.*
>
> ROMANS 5:8

Until You Call Me Home

Lord, I long to be a reflection of You.
Until You call me home, help me to bless Your name.
Be magnified and glorified with every breath I take.

Even when I find myself broken and frightened by the
circumstances in my life, fill me with a longing for
the things that are not of this world.
When the weight of life's burdens drain me, help me to
cast all my worry and fear upon You because You
care for me.
Lord, help me to slow down and find rest in Your loving
arms.
Teach me how to surrender what I cannot keep and
cling to the promises that are mine forever.

Lord, fix my heart on the heavenly treasure that awaits
all of Your children.
In You there is a peace beyond understanding that heals
my soul.

There is hope beyond this life, beyond this moment.
Until You call, help me to focus on the guarantee of
    what is to come.
What You have in store is far more wonderful than
    anything I have ever known.

Woven deep within me is a fierce longing to be with You.
To walk the streets of gold, holding Your hand.
To drink deeply the living water that flows from Your
    glorious throne.
Oh Lord, to taste and see Your goodness.
To be at home.

You have already determined my days here on earth;
You have decreed the exact number of months I will live
    and have set limits that I cannot exceed.
You give me every breath and provide for all my needs,
    yet heaven calls my name.
When I finally make it home, what a day that will be.
Thank You for giving me so much to look forward to.

Praise be to the God and Father of our Lord Jesus
Christ! In his great mercy he has given us new birth
into a living hope through the resurrection of Jesus
Christ from the dead, and into an inheritance
that can never perish, spoil or fade—kept in

*heaven for you, who through faith are shielded
by God's power until the coming salvation
that is ready to be revealed in the last time.*

1 Peter 1:3-5

Greater Love

Why does love hurt so much?
The pain of love isolates me.
Lord, I'm scared to love deeply again.
I don't want to have to say goodbye.
I don't want to hurt anymore.
My gaping heart needs You.

Please reach down and touch me.

Love can be so risky and chaotic, even dangerous.
I try so hard to guard my heart.
Protect it.
Hide it.
Keep it from suffering even more.
I spend myself trying to keep my heart from breaking
    into pieces that can't possibly be put back together
    again.

Please show me what You want from me, Lord.

Are You testing me?

Take what You see and mold me to reflect You better.

Throw away the pieces of this lump of clay that stiff-
arm You.

Burn away the impurities that hinder Your love from
penetrating the hurting areas in my life.

Probe my heart and mind, Lord.

If there's no other way, please crush me into a million
pieces for Your glory.

Show me how to love again so I can be free to let Your
love flow through me.

Help me to love You with all my heart, soul, mind, and
strength.

Tears of anguish drive me into Your embrace, where
Your arms are always open and I am always
welcome.

You love me despite all my inadequacies and offenses.

Because loving me is not about me—it's about You.

It's about who You are.

You risked it all to love me and display a love so grand.

Lord, help me to risk it all to love You back.

> *Greater love has no one than this, that*
> *he lay down his life for his friends.*
>
> JOHN 15:13

122

The Present

I hate when I feel as though I'm waiting for the other
    shoe to drop.
I always feel that something terrible is lurking around
    the corner of my life.
It threatens to disrupt everything.
It longs to steal my comfort.
With much arrogance I cry out, "Haven't I gone
    through enough? Haven't I already experienced
    enough pain and despair in this life?"

Oh God, look what fear has done to me.
I've become a slave to my idea of what this life should
    be like.
I've allowed my broken heart and frayed edges to
    confuse me.
Forgive me, Father.
I hate when life starts to unravel and I reach for worldly
    remedies that will never satisfy.
Please fix my broken thinking.
I'm hurting.

You are the only one that can captivate my affections.

And You are not holding out on me.

You have given me everything I could ever need or want for life and godliness.

You have given me Jesus!

Keep the innermost core of who I am vigilant and steadfast.

I want to be able to say, as Job did, "Though he slay me, yet will I hope in him" (Job 13:15).

Help me to live in the moment and enjoy the gift of the present.

It's all I've been given, and I long to honor You with it.

You alone are the LORD. You made the heavens,
even the highest heavens, and all their starry
host, the earth and all that is on it, the seas and
all that is in them. You give life to everything,
and the multitudes of heaven worship you.

NEHEMIAH 9:6

Safe

No matter what's going on around me and in me, I am
  safe with You.
I'm safe in You.
You are the place I run to, the place where I hide.
The place where nothing and no one can hurt me.
The place where I am fully known and accepted.
You are always safe.

When I don't know where to go or what to do, I can
  rush to where I know You will be.
When I don't have the words and my mind is cluttered
  with fear, I can seek You and find You.
You are not far from me.
You will not hide Your face from me.
You are near to the brokenhearted.
You are always with me. I am never alone.

Because You are safe, I can be who I am.
I don't have to pretend.

125

You have chosen me and will not reject me.

I will not be dismayed or discouraged. You will
strengthen me and help me. You will uphold me.

As I wait patiently for You to deliver me from this place
of deep sorrow and heartbreak, I will trust You.

I will not be anxious or fret.

I will come to You when I am weary and burdened,
and You will give me rest. In You I find rest for my
wounded soul.

Because You are able to do beyond what I can fully
comprehend, I will wait for You, and in Your
perfect timing all will be made new.

You are the Good Shepherd. You gather Your lambs in
Your mighty, loving arms and carry them.

You carry me close to Your heart, where I am held in
the palm of Your hand.

You will protect me and keep me safe.

I am safe in You.

In the day of trouble he will keep me safe in
his dwelling; he will hide me in the shelter of
his tabernacle and set me high upon a rock.

PSALM 27:5

Unseen

You see it all, Lord.
You see the full tapestry of my life and how it's woven
together.
You see the peaks and valleys, the exposed and the
hidden, the beautiful and the ugly, the tears and the
joy.

You see it all.
The intricate details of everything.
You already know how this will all turn out.
You are already there.

"My thoughts are not your thoughts, neither are
your ways my ways," declares the LORD. "As the
heavens are higher than the earth, so are my ways
higher than your ways and my thoughts than your
thoughts" (Isaiah 55:8-9).

Oh Lord, this is great news!

Your ways and thoughts are beyond comprehension;
    they are too awesome for me to understand.
I can trust in what I don't know.
I can trust what I do not see.

You make the crooked straight.
You turn ashes into beauty. You strengthen the weak
    and mend the broken.
You are the giver of life and hope, peace and joy.
You are working it all out for good.
Oh Lord, thank You.
Thank You for being the keeper of the unseen.

> *We fix our eyes not on what is seen, but*
> *on what is unseen. For what is seen is*
> *temporary, but what is unseen is eternal.*
>
> 2 Corinthians 4:18

A Life Worthy

Heavenly Father, I come to You shattered and in
desperate need.

Lord, I'm asking that You would fill me with the
knowledge of Your will through all spiritual
wisdom and understanding.

Keep me from seeking wisdom outside Your truth.

Keep me from trying to understand what is impossible
for me to grasp.

Keep my heart and mind humble before You.

I pray these things so that I may live a life worthy of
You, Lord.

Jesus, even though it seems as though I have nothing to
give, I offer You my pain. I give You all I have.

I pray that I might please You in every way; bearing
fruit in every good work, growing in the knowledge
of who You are.

Please strengthen me right now, Lord, with all power
according to Your glorious might, so that I may

have great hope, increased endurance, and lasting
patience.
Cover me with Your shield so that I can joyfully give
You thanks and praise, even when life isn't going as
I had planned and hoped.

Thank You for rescuing me from the dominion of
darkness and the hopelessness of my deepest fears.
Thank You for bringing me into the kingdom of
Your Son, whom You love and in whom I have
redemption and forgiveness of sins.
Father, thank You for Jesus. Help me to live a life
worthy of all that I am and have.

*I urge you to live a life worthy of the calling you
have received. Be completely humble and gentle;
be patient, bearing with one another in love.*

EPHESIANS 4:2

(A portion of this prayer is taken from Colossians 1:9-14.)

Standing Firm

You have not left me defenseless in my time of great
   need.
You are my defender and protector.
Because You are my help, I am confident and hopeful.
Help me to be strong in You, Lord, and in Your mighty
   power.
I put on the full armor of God and trust You so that I
   can stand firm against the devil's schemes.
My struggle is not against flesh and blood or those who
   come against me and hurt me deeply.
My life and circumstances are in Your capable hands.
Though the rulers, authorities, and powers of this dark
   world and the spiritual forces of evil in the heavenly
   realms want to destroy me, You are God. And I am
   Yours.

Therefore, I put on the full armor of God so that I can
   stand my ground as this war is being waged against
   me.

I put on…
…the helmet of salvation to protect my mind.
I have the mind of Christ Jesus.

…the breastplate of righteousness to protect my heart.
Lord, purify my heart and cleanse me from
    unrighteousness.
When my heart is tempted to stray because of its
    brokenness, please draw me back into Your limitless
    love.
Create in me a pure heart and renew a passion for all
    that is true within me.

…the belt of truth.
I will not listen to any lies from the enemy nor tell any
    lies.
I will listen and bend my heart to the voice of truth.
Jesus, You are my truth.

…boots fitted with the gospel of peace.
Wherever I go, Lord, help me to bring the good news.
Even when my heart is on the mend and true joy seems
    so far way, help me to be a beacon of light wherever
    You take me.

…the shield of faith that extinguishes all the fiery darts
    of the enemy.

Lord, please increase my faith when the concerns in
my life and the cares of this world try to weigh me
down.

...and the sword of the Spirit, which is Your Word.
Please hide Your Word in my heart so that I will not sin
against You.
Lord, especially when my heart is heavy and burdened,
please bury Your Word deep within me.

*Finally, be strong in the Lord and in his mighty
power. Put on the full armor of God so that you
can take your stand against the devil's schemes.*
Ephesians 6:10-11

(A portion of this prayer is taken from Ephesians 6:10-18.)

My First Love

Oh Lord, be my first love.
All that I am and all that I have are Yours.
Increase my passion and desire for You.
Why do I yearn for what can never satisfy?
Why do I look beyond Your tender arms for love and
    security?

You are my satisfaction.
Help me to want nothing more than more of You.
Keep my wandering heart from going astray.
You are the answer to all my hopes and dreams.

You are everything!
You see the depths of who I am and You love me
    anyway.
Help me to be content in You.
Fill my emptiness, Lord.
Please continue to break down the walls of bondage
    around my heart.

Keep me far from unforgiveness and bitterness.

You are the lover of my soul.
Your love reaches into my deepest pain and revives me.
Nothing and no one compares to You.
I'm alive in Your love.

We love because he first loved us.

1 JOHN 4:19

Treasure of My Heart

I have not always treasured You in my heart.
I have tried to fill my life with this world and the many
  things that cannot satisfy my yearning soul.
I have searched for satisfaction and fulfillment apart
  from You, and I have been left broken and empty,
  disillusioned and distraught.
I have treasured and craved my own comfort more than
  Your presence.

Oh Father, forgive me.
I lacked wisdom, but You gave generously to me even
  though I did not deserve it.
I needed guidance, and You instructed me and showed
  me the way to go. You counseled me and watched
  over me.
In my weakness, Your grace was sufficient and Your
  power was made perfect.

Lord, thank You for always making a way for me to run
back to You.
Thank You for the forgiveness and restoration I find in
You alone.
I need You.
Lord, You are so good to me.
I am Your treasured possession.
How can that be?
Though You see the depths and motives of my heart,
You love me anyway.
You are amazing!
God, You are faithful to all Your promises and loving
toward all You have made.
You uphold me when I fall and lift me up when I am
bowed down.

I will sing of Your love, faithfulness, and greatness, for
You are my fortress, my refuge in times of trouble...
my loving, compassionate God.
Lord, be my heart's desire and treasure.

Where your treasure is, there your heart will be also.
Matthew 6:21

Guard My Mind and Heart

This place of anguish and brokenness is horrible.
I feel consumed by sorrow and loneliness.
My mind is being assaulted by the enemy of my soul.
My faith is being hammered with doubt.

Come to my rescue, Lord.
Please keep me from being led astray.
Please protect me from being swallowed up by self-pity
    and disappointment.
Please bless me with discernment, and help me to be
    watchful and aware of the enemy's schemes.

Holy Spirit, renew my mind and let Your peace, which
    surpasses all understanding rule in and guard my
    heart.
Demolish everything that sets itself up against the
    knowledge I have of You and who You are in all
    Your glory.

And please, Lord, help me to take captive every thought that is not in line with the truth.

Father, when I feel as though the pieces of my life will never be made whole, please remind me that You began a good work in me and You will be faithful to complete it.

Set my mind and heart on things above, where my Savior, Jesus, is seated at Your right hand.

For I am Yours. My life is hidden with Christ.

In my weakness, when the brokenness of my life tries to drain me of all joy and life, You are my salvation.

You will keep me strong until the end.

You see my misery.

You hear me when I cry.

You know what I need during this time of heartbreak.

And You will come down and rescue me and draw me close to Your heart.

Please help me to focus on what is true and noble, right and pure, lovely and admirable, honorable, praiseworthy and excellent.

Fix my heart on You, Jesus, for You are the Lover of my soul and the Author and Finisher of my faith.

*Do not conform any longer to the pattern
of this world, but be transformed by the
renewing of your mind. Then you will be
able to test and approve what God's will
is—his good, pleasing and perfect will.*

Romans 12:2

When I Call

When I call out to You, You hear me and give ear to my
    prayers.
"In my distress I called to the LORD; I cried to my God
    for help. From his temple he heard my voice; my cry
    came before him, into his ears" (Psalm 18:6).

You see the depth of my need and deliver me.
You bend down, brush away my tears, and treasure each
    one.

You listen and answer my pleas.
You comfort and keep me.

When the enemy tries to rob me of all peace and life,
    You reach down and save me.
You watch over my life when the depth of my troubles
    runs deep.

"You, O LORD, keep my lamp burning; my God turns
    my darkness into light" (Psalm 18:28).

When I reach out for You, You are there.
You draw me in to where I am fully known and loved
    beyond measure.
Your presence is life to me.

When I call You are always there for me.
I don't know what I would do without You.

> *The Lord is my rock, my fortress and my deliverer;*
> *my God is my rock, in whom I take refuge. He*
> *is my shield and the horn of my salvation, my*
> *stronghold. I call to the Lord, who is worthy*
> *of praise, and I am saved from my enemies.*
>
> PSALM 18:2-3

Joy Will Come

Joy will come, of this I am certain.
Even though in these moments I can't see beyond my
    pain, I believe that joy will come.
It will because You promised.
"Those who sow in tears will reap with songs of joy"
    (Psalm 126:5).

With these trials a sense of anticipation, wrapped in
    great hope, helps me to persevere.
When I don't know what to do, Your peace, which
    is beyond understanding, fills me in ways
    indescribable.
The joy of the Lord is my strength.
You cover me and keep me in Your loving presence.

For as deep as this heart-wrenching season takes me, I
    know that You are there. You are deeper still.
Your love and compassion will never leave me.

I will enter into the peace of Your presence as I rest in
   You.
You are my joy and delight now and forever.

"I am still confident of this: I will see the goodness of
   the LORD in the land of the living. Wait for the
   LORD; be strong and take heart and wait for the
   LORD" (Psalm 27:13-14).
Because You are, joy will come again.
It will.

> *You turned my wailing into dancing; you removed*
>   *my sackcloth and clothed me with joy, that*
>   *my heart may sing to you and not be silent. O*
>   *LORD my God, I will give you thanks forever.*
>
> PSALM 30:11-12

When I Look at You

Jesus, You are amazing.
When I look at You, the truth of who You are changes
   everything.
It changes the way I live and breathe.
It changes how I deal with the circumstances I find
   myself in right now.
It changes me.

When I look at You, I see myself for who I really am.
I see my desperate need for a Savior and Redeemer.
I see my weaknesses being covered in Your mighty
   strength.
I see the shadows of despair and depression being lifted.

I find a hope that is real, a love that endures, and
   promises that are fulfilled when I look at You.
Jesus, please keep my heart and mind fixed on what is
   true.
The past is over, and You hold this moment.

You hold it all together for Your glory and divine
    purpose.
You hold me.

When I look at You, Breath of Heaven, my heart is
    filled with a hope that helps me to persevere.
A hope that encourages me to praise and honor You in
    this storm.
A hope that fills me with life.
You are my hope.

> *I will praise the* LORD, *who counsels me; even
> at night my heart instructs me. I have set the
> LORD always before me. Because he is at my right
> hand, I will not be shaken. Therefore my heart
> is glad and my tongue rejoices; my body will rest
> secure, because…you have made known to me
> the path of life; you will fill me with joy in your
> presence, with eternal pleasures at your right hand.*
>
> PSALM 16:7-11

Who Is Like You?

From the intricate magnificence of an infant forming
in a mother's womb to the sprawling heavens with
their billions of shimmering galaxies nestled in the
night skies, You spoke and it was...

From the fierce seas, their waves foaming in power
against the shoreline, to the splendor of creation's
majesty, rainbows, shooting stars, and animals great
and small,
You spoke and it was...

And here I am in the midst of it all, facedown and
longing for a tender touch from Your hand.
Longing for Your gentle voice to soothe the pain in my
heart.
Longing to lay my head upon Your chest, where my
cries are heard by You.
To breathe in sync with Your divine heartbeat and
behold You and Your glory in this place of sorrow.

How is it that even in my darkness I know that my
    Redeemer lives, and that in the end He will stand
    upon this earth?
Oh, how my heart and soul yearn deep within me.

While I wait for deliverance to come, You offer Your
    heart, to comfort me.
Because You alone are the remedy for my brokenness.
You, the Mighty God, in whom the fullness of all
    majesty, power, and glory resides, You commanded
    the universe to be, and You chose to have Your heart
    broken so that in You my heart can be made whole.
My heart can be healed and made new.
Without You being fragile and willing, I would never
    be able to run to You with my vulnerability and
    trust that You know and care.
Who is like You?

> *Can you fathom the mysteries of God? Can*
> *you probe the limits of the Almighty? They are*
> *higher than the heavens—what can you do?*
> *They are deeper than the depths of the grave—*
> *what can you know? Their measure is longer*
> *than the earth and wider than the sea.*

JOB 11:7-9

I Don't Want to Hurt Anymore

Those days, Lord, I have so many of them.
I am overwhelmed by heaviness and I can't help but just
    fall apart.
It seems my dreams burst into flames, turn to ashes,
    and blustery winds of change carry them off, right
    out of my hands, and then they are gone…forever.

Must I have days like this?
Days where my heart breaks, tears fall, and I become so
    frustrated with everything?

Must I feel this way?
I long for my heart to be warmed by the fire of Your
    deep abiding grace.
I need to hear You singing:

"The Lord your God is with you, he is mighty to save.

He will take great delight in you, he will quiet you with his love, he will rejoice over you with singing" (Zephaniah 3:17).

I plead for You to quiet me with Your love.
I don't want my hurt to push You away but draw me closer to You.
I come with heaviness, mourning, and ashes; weeping rivers of tears as I hold out my torn heart to You and cry out, "Please take me as I am."
I look down, only to see the ground beneath my feet.
I search for You everywhere.

I stagger about, hoping that healing will come.
And then I remember that Your arms are outstretched, as far as the east is from the west, so great is Your love and compassion toward me.
My eyes gaze upon the incredible beauty of Your love, ablaze for me and for all who would put their hope in You.
And I look to the cross, where Your precious heart called out my name.
This is where I run when I don't want to hurt anymore.
Into Your mercy that covers my every need.
I love You.

*I call to God and the LORD saves me. Evening,
morning and noon I cry out in distress and
he hears my voice. He ransoms me unharmed
from the battle waged against me.*

PSALM 55:16-18

What More Can I Do?

I've done all I can.
I've prayed until my knees are calloused.
I've loved until my heart is threadbare.
I've given until I've scraped the bottom.
I've reached out until my arms ache and my soul throbs.

What more can I do, Lord?
I'm willing, but I feel so empty and useless.
You know my heart.
You see that I have done all that I can.
Now what?

My armor is beaten and worn.
I'm having trouble fighting the good fight.
My faith seems so ragged and lame.
I need You to engage the enemy and push back the
    powers of darkness on my behalf.
Please fight for me.

Oh Lord, fill me with courage…the courage to turn the
other cheek!

The courage to love those who despise me and hurt me.

The courage to resist locking the doors, closing the
shades, and running the other way when my life
unravels.

What more can I do but surrender my life and trust that
all will be well?

Help me to stand firm and let nothing move me.

No matter what's going on in my life, help me to always
give myself fully to all You would have me do in
this world, because I know and believe with all my
heart that a life lived for You is not lived in vain.

And so I choose to live for You, believing that even my
trail of tears

Is not in vain.

Be on your guard; stand firm in the
faith; be men of courage; be strong.
1 Corinthians 16:13

Louder Than Words

I'm sorry, Lord. I blew it again.
Why is it so easy to call You "Lord" and yet not live as
   though I believe the things You say?

My actions really do speak louder than words, and what
   I say with my life sometimes drowns out what I say
   with my mouth.
I proclaim to trust You, but when I look in the mirror,
   all I see is fear and doubt.

Why is it so easy to push You off the throne of my
   heart?
To believe the lies bombarding my mind?
To seek what cannot satisfy?
To wallow in self-sufficiency?

Why do I do this to myself?

I feel so tender and fragile, so easily torn.

Why do I contend with what I know to be true?
I am Your beloved!
You have given me abundant life and shown me
    kindness, compassion, and mercy.
Lord, in Your great providence each and every day You
    watch over my spirit.
No temptation has seized me except what is common
    to man.
And You are faithful. You will not let me be tempted
    beyond what I can bear.
But when I am tempted, You will provide a way out for
    me.

Though I have pleaded for You to take this thorn in the
    flesh from me, I choose to smile through tear-filled
    eyes.
As You open Your arms and welcome me as I am, I see
    afresh that Your grace and love are sufficient.

When You look deep into my soul, at the very things I
    long to hide, I know I am loved beyond reason.

When You take my trembling hand, I fall into Your
    warm, winsome heart and feel safe.
Your embrace teaches me to be still.

And as I quiet myself before You, I hear You whisper
with a love louder than words, "I love you."

I will boast all the more gladly about my weaknesses,
so that Christ's power may rest on me. That is
why, for Christ's sake, I delight in weaknesses, in
insults, in hardships, in persecutions, in difficulties.
For when I am weak, then I am strong.

2 Corinthians 12:9-10

Pray

The battle rages, fierce and relentless, tearing me to
    pieces.

My flesh longs for comfort and ease.
My mind sifts through the clutter, parroting a muddled
    to-do list that grows long enough to cover my fridge.
I need to be quiet.
I need rest.
You never guaranteed that life would be easy, but You
    did promise to hear when we call.

Why is praying so hard?
Lord, why is it such a knock-down, drag-out battle with
    the world, the flesh, and the enemy?

Sometimes when I fall to my knees, nothing will come
    out.
I'm speechless.
Yet I believe that the Spirit is there for me.

"In the same way, the Spirit helps us in our weakness.
 We do not know what we ought to pray for, but the
 Spirit himself intercedes for us with groans that
 words cannot express" (Romans 8:26).
I am comforted by this truth.
When I pray, I'm lifted beyond time and grasp eternity.
You know what I need before I ask.
So I leave the to-do list for later to fall at Your feet, lay
 my head in Your lap, cry, cleave to You, and feel
 Your heartbeat.

You lift up my head and gird me for battle.
In prayer I come boldly before the throne of grace,
 obtaining mercy and finding help.
Please continue to teach me how to pray.

*We do not have a high priest who is unable to
sympathize with our weaknesses, but we have one
who has been tempted in every way, just as we are—
yet was without sin. Let us then approach the throne
of grace with confidence, so that we may receive
mercy and find grace to help us in our time of need.*

Hebrews 4:15-16

You Are My Rescue

"Praise be to the LORD my Rock…He is my loving God
    and my fortress, my stronghold and my deliverer,
    my shield, in whom I take refuge" (Psalm 144:1-2).

I have nowhere else to go but into Your arms.
There's nowhere else I'd rather be than close to where I
    can hear Your heartbeat.
I hide myself in Your unfailing love.

The crushing weight I find myself under right now is
    not too heavy for You.
I can't carry this burden…but You can and You will.
You have shown me such kindness, and You have kept
    me from falling.
In the shadows I can still see Your light shine forth like
    the dawn.
The snare set before me will cause me no harm because
    You are with me and You will keep me from
    stumbling.

Though this anguish continues to bring me down, Your
peace will be my comfort.
You will rescue me because You love me.
"In my distress I called to the LORD, and he answered
me. From the depths of the grave I called for help,
and you listened to my cry" (Jonah 2:2).
When I was on my knees, crying out to You in my sea
of pain, You reached down and grabbed hold of me.
Thank You, Lord.
Your goodness overwhelms me.

> *He reached down from on high and took hold of*
> *me; he drew me out of deep waters. He rescued*
> *me from my powerful enemy, from my foes, who*
> *were too strong for me. They confronted me in*
> *the day of my disaster, but the LORD was my*
> *support. He brought me out into a spacious place;*
> *he rescued me because he delighted in me.*
>
> PSALM 18:16-19

Letting Go

I try so hard to hang on.
But I need to let go.
I need to let go of trying to hold on to anything other
    than the hope I have in You, Jesus.
You are enough.
You are all I need.
You are sufficient.

Help me to let go.
Help me to let go of unforgiveness so that I can gain a
    heart of forgiveness.
Keep me from hanging on to the past so that I can
    embrace the present and anticipate the future.
Help me to let go of what I had hoped for so that I can
    fully embrace the better plan and purpose You have
    for my life.
I'm so tired of hanging on.
Please give me the strength to release my life into Your
    hands.

Help me to surrender all and cling to You alone.

Lord, I don't want to miss out on You because I'm so
wrapped up in me.
Please pull back the layers of my heart and purify me.
Cleanse me from all that would hinder me from seeing
You at work in the midst of this pain.
Father, Your Son was pierced for me. He endured
unimaginable pain so that I could run to You with
everything.

Help me to let go…and let You be God in every area of
my life.
Take all of me.
Have Your way, Lord. Have Your way.

*Brothers, I do not consider myself yet to have taken
hold of it. But one thing I do: Forgetting what
is behind and straining toward what is ahead, I
press on toward the goal to win the prize for which
God has called me heavenward in Christ Jesus.*

Philippians 3:13

Everything Beautiful

Oh Lord, I long for the unfading beauty of a gentle and
quiet spirit, which is of great worth in Your sight.
Keep anger and frustration far from me as I navigate
through this brokenness.
Quiet me with Your love and gentleness when I want to
let loose.

I'm so sad.
Yet my soul still sings of Your love and greatness. The
beauty of who You are still shines forth through the
darkness.
I'm drawn to the deep well of life that I find only in You.
When this is all said and done, when You rescue me
from this place, I will have scars.
But my scars are beautiful to You.
Though most of my wounds are hidden deep within my
heart, You see them.
You were wounded and afflicted for me.
You were pierced for my transgressions and crushed for

my iniquities; the punishment that brought peace into my life was upon You and because of Your wounds I am healed.

"Though you have made me see troubles, many and bitter, you will restore my life again; from the depths of the earth you will again bring me up. You will increase my honor and comfort me once again" (Psalm 71:21-22).

There is a beauty in store I have yet to see and experience.
A beauty beyond my tears and fears.
An unfathomable beauty that will captivate and consume me for all eternity.
An unquenchable beauty that will endure.
I can hardly wait, Lord.

He has made everything beautiful in its time. He has also set eternity in the hearts of men; yet they cannot fathom what God has done from beginning to end.

ECCLESIASTES 3:11

In You I Am Home

❧

"Lord, you have been our dwelling place throughout
   all generations. Before the mountains were born
   or you brought forth the earth and the world,
   from everlasting to everlasting you are God"
   (Psalm 90:1-2).
In You, I am safe, I am home.
I start and end in You.

This moment, this life, is a vapor.
I am here today and gone tomorrow.
The troubles of this world and the concerns on my heart
   will be no more.
All will be made new.

I will be home at last.
I will be in Your presence for all eternity, where time
   does not exist.
Who can fathom this?

Who can comprehend what it will be like to see You
     face-to-face?
Just the thought of it overwhelms me.

I long to be with You where I am fully Yours.
I crave the perfection and beauty of my heavenly home.
I delight in the thought of worshipping You with a pure
     heart and mind.
I rejoice that every day is one day closer to that day.
I'm desperate for You, Jesus.

While I wait, please help me to be mindful that I'm
     home in You now.
As I anticipate what's to come, I can rest in You now.
You are not far from me at all, for in You I live, move,
     and have my being.
Thank You, Jesus.

> *Our citizenship is in heaven. And we eagerly*
> *await a Savior from there, the Lord Jesus Christ.*
>
> Philippians 3:20

Rejoice in the Suffering

Lord, You never guaranteed this life would be free from troubles.

You never said the journey would be easy.

You never promised a life free from strife and suffering.

So why am I surprised?

Why do I meander through this difficult season of life disillusioned and confused?

Why does this moment of deep trouble shock me so?

You told us we would have trials.

You told us tribulations would come upon us, that suffering would be a part of this life.

"I have told you these things, so that in me you may have peace. In this world you will have trouble. But take heart! I have overcome the world" (John 16:33).

You told us...but You also promised to be with us in the midst of the torrent.

You promised to protect us.

"When you pass through the waters, I will be with you; and when you pass through the rivers, they will not sweep over you. When you walk through the fire, you will not be burned; the flames will not set you ablaze. For I am the LORD, your God, the Holy One of Israel, your Savior" (Isaiah 43:2-3).

Therefore, my heart will rejoice during this painful trial because You are with me.

Because I am Yours, no weapon formed against me shall prosper.

Though You have allowed the circumstances in my life to be as they are right now, in this moment I will trust You.

Your grace is enough.

Your ways are perfect, higher, better though mysterious and beyond understanding.

I will rejoice during this my season because I trust and believe that this suffering will produce in me perseverance, character, and hope. This great and lasting hope that I have in You, Jesus, will not disappoint because You have poured out Your love into my heart by the Holy Spirit, whom You have given me.

Help me to remember that my heartbreak and present sufferings are not worth comparing to the glory that will be revealed in me.

You are my hiding place, my comfort in all my troubles.
For just as Your sufferings flow over into my life, so
    because of You, because of Your mercy, Your grace
    and comfort overflow into my life…into this
    moment.

Oh Father, I long to suffer well.
I long to bring You glory even now, in the midst of all
    that's going on, in the middle of this place.
When I have come to the end of this heartbreak, more
    than anything I pray that as a result of this time in
    the valley that You will be magnified above my pain.
That it was You…You shone forth in the midst of it all.

> *Dear friends, do not be surprised at the painful
> trial you are suffering, as though something
> strange were happening to you. But rejoice that
> you participate in the sufferings of Christ, so that
> you may be overjoyed when his glory is revealed.*
>
> 1 PETER 4:12-14

Enduring Love

There is a love that endures.
A love that stands the test of time and heartbreak.
A love that reaches beyond my limited ability to fully
    comprehend and embrace.
A love that understands and knows me.
A love that sees the depths of my heart and loves me
    anyway.

There is a love that is lavish and extravagant.
A love that covers all wrongs and makes the
    unrighteous holy.
A love that lives out loud and hides nothing in shame.
A love that dies for the sinner and saves the wicked.
A love that reaches as far as the east is from the west,
    and as high as the heavens are from the earth.

There is a great love that is winsome and joyful, happy,
    and contagious.
A love that satisfies the needy and mends the broken.

The kind of love that forgives and forgets, heals and
makes whole.
An abounding love that is always dependable and true.
A love that wraps itself around you and changes
everything.

Lord, You are love.
Because of Your unfailing love, I have everything I
need.
I cry out to You in the midst of this disaster, and You
send forth from heaven and save me. You send Your
love and faithfulness and help me to endure.
"I will be glad and rejoice in your love, for you saw my
affliction and knew the anguish of my soul" (Psalm
31:7).

You will preserve and protect my life according to Your
unshakable love.
Help me to walk in love even now as I look to You and
trust You with all that concerns me.

*Great is your love toward me; you have
delivered me from the depths of the grave.*

Psalm 86:13

Victory Will Come

Lord, I don't want to just endure this trouble. I long to have victory as a result of it.

In the midst of this time of testing, I pray You will be glorified.

In You alone victory is found.

Reveal in and through me a greater hope and peace that conquers all.

Help me stand firm and trust You, especially when I have no clue as to what You are doing.

When doubt and fear creep in on my faith, strengthen my walk and give me wisdom.

I run to You with the unfulfilled longings of my heart and cravings of my soul.

Though I am unworthy, You take me as I am and love me.

You will fight for me against the darkness of this world.

You will shoulder the burdens trying to pull me into the grave.

The radiance of Your truth will guide me and I will not
  be moved.
I will stand firm.

I will be victorious.
Not because I am strong, but because in my weakness,
  Jesus, You are strong.
Victory rests in You alone.
My confidence is in You.
The longing for You to be extraordinary in the midst of
  this trial consumes me.
Make Yourself known, Jesus.
Rescure me from the depths of my brokenness and
  show Yourself mighty.
So that all will see and know that You are God.
Victory in You is certain.
Thank You, Lord.

*Thanks be to God! He gives us the victory through
our Lord Jesus Christ. Therefore, my dear brothers,
stand firm. Let nothing move you. Always give
yourselves fully to the work of the Lord, because you
know that your labor in the Lord is not in vain.*

1 Corinthians 15:57-58

Help Me to Persevere

I need You, Lord.

Please help me to consider it pure joy whenever I face
trials of many kinds.

Help me to know that the testing of my faith develops
perseverance, a perseverance that must finish its
work so that I may be mature and complete, not
lacking anything.

This is so hard.

The gaping hole in my heart is swallowing up all my joy.

Please move this mountain, Lord.

Snatch me from the fire of my affliction.

Turn this heap of ashes into a beauty that I have never
known.

Help me.

I try to mask my pain but it continues to intrude in on
my life when I least expect it.

Where is my faith?

Where is my confidence?

Though I walk in the midst of trouble, You preserve my
life; You stretch out Your hand and save me. You
will not abandon me when I need You most.
I will not trust in the flesh.
My hope is not in what mortal man can do.
My hope is in You.
My life and times are hidden in the affection and love
of an all-knowing, gracious, almighty God.
You sustain me.
The chaos of my life is held in Your perfect peace.

I will say with confidence, "The Lord is my helper; I
will not be afraid."
For Your sake, Lord Jesus, I delight in my weaknesses…
my hardships, pain, and difficulties.
For when I am weak, because of You alone I am strong.
Thank You for helping me to press on when I want to
give up.
Thank You for helping me to give in to Your perfect
plans in the middle of these trials.

Blessed is the man who perseveres under
trial, because when he has stood the test, he
will receive the crown of life that God
has promised to those who love him.

JAMES 1:12

As I Am

I can't stay here anymore.
I can't stand this mess of a life.
I want to run away from it all.
Far away from the pain that entangles me in despair
    and grief.
I want to run from myself.

I'm needy.
Frustrated.
Confused.
Angry.
Flawed.

I'm a complete mess.

It's time for a change.
It's time to move on.
It's time to stop wrestling, stop doubting, and just believe.
It's time for me to walk in the purpose for which You
    have created me.

But what about my broken heart?
What about this ache that lingers?
What shall I do about this anguish of soul that follows
    me around like my shadow?
Where do I put the tears?
Where can I hide that is safe?
Lord, what do I do with me?

My life is anchored to Your unrelenting goodness and
    grace.
Your mercy keeps me and transforms this mess into
    something beautiful.
Your love paid the price for my freedom—for my
    life—so that in You I come as I am.

With all my heart, soul, mind, and strength, I press in
    to You.
I surrender my tattered self and trust You with all that
    I am.
Because no matter what, You love me as I am.

You love me.

May your unfailing love be my comfort,
according to your promise to your servant.
Let your compassion come to me that I
may live, for your law is my delight.

Psalm 119:76-77

Waiting

It feels as though I've been waiting for so long.
Sometimes I sense that doubt and fear are trying to
    invade my mind as I wait for You, Lord.
As I cling to You during these moments of longing, help
    me to remember that You are in control.
You are already there.
You already know.
It's all good.
Because You are God and You are good.

While I wait for You, help me to be still.
Help me to trust and know that You are at work in the
    midst of my pain.
Help me to rest in Your faithfulness as You work this
    all out.
Please strengthen my faith and bless me with greater
    wisdom, Lord.
While I wait, rearrange my thinking and fix my eyes on
    You, Jesus.

Turn my worry and anxious thoughts into prayer and
thanksgiving.
Help me to surrender to Your sovereignty over all that
concerns me right now.
You have not left me alone to fend for myself.
You are with me even now as I cry out to You in my
distress.
Please keep me from letting my impatience get the best
of me.
I don't want to be impatient. I want to trust You fully.

While I wait, keep my heart and mind focused on You
rather than on the outcome of my circumstances.
This is hard, and I can't do it on my own.
I need You to fix my focus and capture my heart.
You hold the outcome; even more so You hold me.
Lord, more than anything I want the desire of my heart
to be You.
Not what You can do…
Just You.
Jesus, You are worth waiting for.

*Wait for the LORD; be strong and take
heart and wait for the LORD.*

PSALM 27:14

Beyond This

Beyond the tears…
Beyond the pain…
Beyond the darkness…
There is a place being prepared for me.

Where there is no mourning or sorrow, no sin or hiding,
    no hopelessness or shame.

The old order of things is no more.
Oh, what a day that will be!
Your gracious provision will overwhelm me like a flood,
    and I will want for nothing but You.
You will be the desire of my heart forever.

I will no longer be concerned about the cares of this
    world; all will be made new.
Though I feel entrenched in this season of great sorrow,
    there is hope.
Because of the promises You have made, I press on.

Because of Your great love, this is not the end of the
story.
There is a joy I have never known beyond this.

As life unravels and falls apart all around me, You hold
me still.
You love me and will come back and get me, so that I
can be with You forever.
Thank You for keeping me strong and steadfast until I
see You face-to-face.
You are my hope now and beyond this life.

> *In my Father's house are many rooms; if it were*
> *not so, I would have told you. I am going there to*
> *prepare a place for you. And if I go and prepare*
> *a place for you, I will come back and take you to*
> *be with me that you also may be where I am.*

JOHN 14:2-3

Longing to Be with You

I'm tired of running.
I'm tired of trying to do this in my own strength.
I self-protect to the point of exhaustion.
What in the world am I doing, Lord?
Rescue me from myself.

I can't do it.
I give up.
I'm done with this life.
I'm so sick of living with this pain.
At times it's unbearable.
Every day I wake up and it's still there.
My tears have been my food both day and night as I cry
     out to You.
As I seek You and call out to You with every breath,
     come quickly, Lord.
Please.
I'm tortured by impatience and longing.
The need to be in Your presence consumes me.

I just want to be with You, Jesus.

Only in Your arms do I find rest.
Joy comes when I quiet myself and allow Your presence
     to comfort me.
Help me to receive the balm of grace Your wounds have
     provided.
Jesus, because of Your stripes, I am healed.

Until You come to take me home, please help me to live.
Help me to radiate the eternal hope You have provided,
     the hope that encourages me to press on.
While I wait to see You, please remind me that You are
     always with me.
You are my now and my forever.

> *Our citizenship is in heaven. And we eagerly await
> a Savior from there, the Lord Jesus Christ, who, by
> the power that enables him to bring everything
> under his control, will transform our lowly
> bodies so that they will be like his glorious body.*
>
> PHILIPPIANS 3:20-21

A New Song

Someday soon, I will sing a new song.
I will dance and praise in the presence of the King, and
I will be glad all of my days.

With a new song on my lips, I will worship in a way that
I never have before.

The justice of God will reign, and the tears of the saints
will be no more.
We will sing a new song.

There will be a day when no more tears will fall from
my eyes and the pain in my heart will be gone.
You will wipe away every tear. There will be no more
death or mourning or crying or pain.
That will all be gone, for the old order of things will
have passed away.

I will see the tapestry of my life and the ways in which

You used every trial and triumph for Your glory and
my good.

I will know You more and nothing will hinder my
relationship with You.

I will see You face-to-face. With excitement and
anticipation I press on until that day.

That day when I will sing with overwhelming joy a new
song.

*I heard a sound from heaven like the roar of
rushing waters and like a loud peal of thunder. The
sound I heard was like that of harpists playing their
harps. And they sang a new song before the throne.*

REVELATION 14:2-3

HUNTER'S HOPE

Please check out the Hunter's Hope website
and Jill Kelly's personal website.
God is good!

www.huntershope.org

www.jillk.org

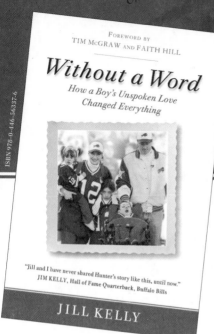

FOREWORD BY
TIM McGRAW and FAITH HILL

Without a Word

*How a Boy's Unspoken Love
Changed Everything*

ISBN 978-0-446-56337-6

"Jill and I have never shared Hunter's story like this, until now."
JIM KELLY, Hall of Fame Quarterback, Buffalo Bills

JILL KELLY

Without
a Word

*How a Boy's
Unspoken Love
Changed Everything*

Without a Word is a riveting memoir that blends remarkable achievement with passion, sacrifice, love, pain and human interest. It takes the reader into the lives of a celebrity couple, pro football Hall of Famer Jim Kelly and his wife, Jill, to reveal the family's private struggle and how eight years with their severely disabled, terminally ill son, Hunter, unfolded in a remarkable story of redemption.

www.faithwords.com

Faith
Words™
A Division of Hachette Book Group